GRATITUDES

Thank you to the following artists for use of their photography:
Emiliano Arano (cover+p52), Pixabay (pp2, 24+76), Harrison Candlin (p5),
Karolina Grabowska (pp8, 14, 15+68), Zak Sheuskaya (pp12+13),
Aistä Sveikataitä (pp16+17), Nika Akin (p20), Aaron Kittredge (p22),
Evie Shaffer (p24), Jan Kopåiva (pp26+27), Lumn (pp38, 40+41),
Mark McCammon (p46), Tomaj Malak (p75), Anni Roenkae (p80)

Thank you to Lisa Muller-Jones for her creativity, collaboration,
graphic design + layout expertise. You are loved.

All other paintings and doodles by Anne L. Davis.

We are energy. Everything in this world is energy including how we feel, what we think, and how we move.

This foundational understanding means that everything is malleable. We are always moving, morphing, changing.

We are in a constant state of vibration.

Since everything is energy, we have an opportunity to move it.

This concept completely changed my perspective on life.

Tool your mind towards
what fuels your imagination.

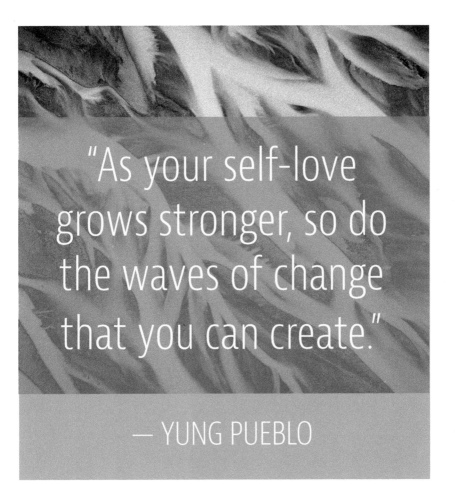

"As your self-love grows stronger, so do the waves of change that you can create."

— YUNG PUEBLO

Any. Way. You. Like.

There are no rules. That said, this journal
follows a path that worked for me!

ON MY PATH I USED:
— Scissors & Glue (or tape)
— 3 rubber bands
— Post-It® notes
— Old magazines
— My body, my voice

Vibe Guide is a framework for:

* Deciding where you want to focus your energy.
* Noticing it.
* Moving it.
* Anchoring it.
* Expressing it.
*...and sometimes letting it go... or morph into something else.

Energy work is **BODY** work. It is movement + creation.

Use this guide in ways that feel right to you. You might color, crinkle the paper, paint it, yell at it, sing it, doodle it, wax poetic on it, rip it all up and start again.

It is a companion on your journey. Make it work for you. **However you like.**

Decide.

Like anything else, if you want to make a change, you need to focus on it.

Take your time
determining what
"a decision"
feels/looks/smells like.

What does it mean to decide?

What does it look like?

How does it feel in your body?

Decide. **DECIDE.** choose...

Decisions can be big or small. You might choose to
keep your heart open. You might choose to notice
when life feels like it flows... or when
things feel stuck.

My heart
is open.

Sometimes a visual is helpful to solidify
a decision.

You could try a manifest board or vision
board **like this...**

< ·

I am good
+ perfect +
kind without
<u>doing</u> anything.

I am safe
in my
body.

...or use Post-Its®!

Sometimes it helps to lock the **choice** into your cells...

Move the **decision** through your body............>

Reach it through your fingertips!

Hands to hips & chin lifts.

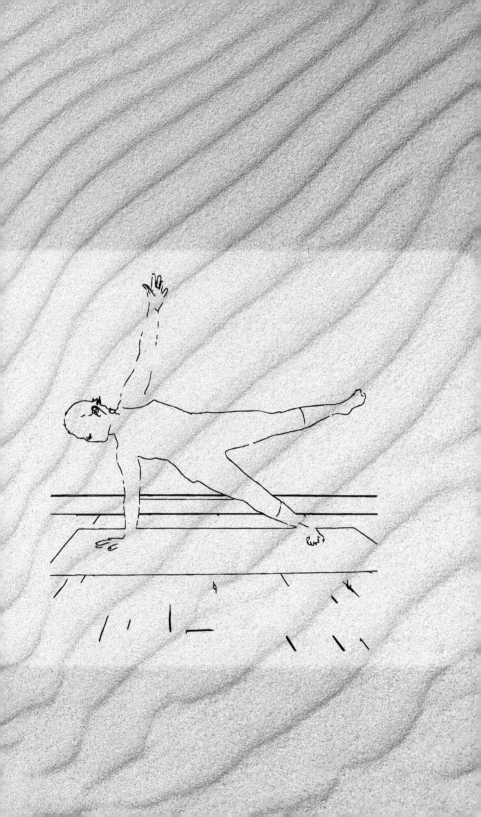

Today, I decide:

write here

HERE'S WHAT WORKED FOR ME:

For me, choosing to love myself meant:
— Creating time & space for me
— Being curious and gentle
— Throwing my shoulders back and
   lifting my heart to the sky

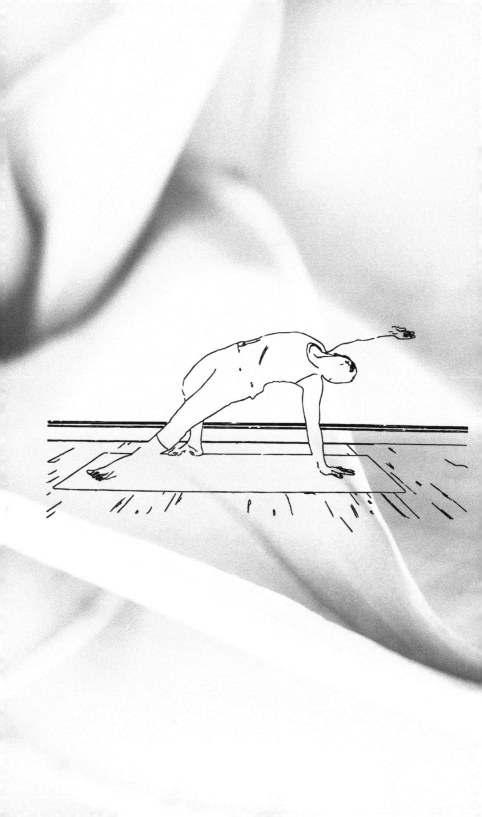

 **OWN** your choice

 write here

It is an act of
rebellION  to love yourself.
You got this.

Shuni Mudra

- Middle finger to thumb
- Generate stability & follow-through on commitments

Bring your decision to your breath.
Press your fingers together and breathe!

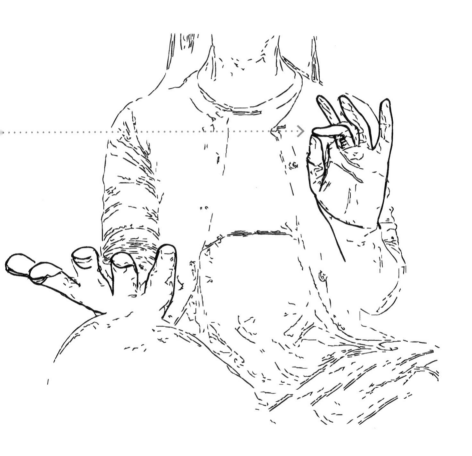

(you can't do it wrong! Phew!!)

Notice.

This phase is all about s–l–o–w–i–n–g down.
And paying attention.

You made your decision; **I choose me!** Nice job!

Now, you may notice what comes up (in your head).
Sometimes, the things that come up aren't so kind.

How do you talk to yourself?

When do you blame or judge yourself?

When do you hide or self-censor?

@ Notice with

kindness, curiosity, & ♡ compassion!!

You don't need to change it ··············>
(or chastise yourself)!

Just NOTICE,
ALLOW ♥
and SOOTHE.

YOU'RE DOING GREAT!!

So...how do I notice??

write here

You can practice by paying attention to your breath.

◎ Breathe in, 2, 3, 4

◎ Breathe out, 2, 3, 4, 5, 6

quiet

the storyline in your mind...

Breathe.

Draw.

Move.

SING.

Color.

COLORING

CHILLS YOU OUT.

Today, I noticed: _____ ✏️

_____

_____

_____

_____

I wonder if: _____

_____

_____

_____

_____

It might be: _____

_____

_____

_____

_____

All I need to do is: _____

_____

_____

_____

_____

GO DO THAT THING!

Ways I **HIDE**

Ways I **JUDGE**

Gratitude ♡

is the root of joy, abundance + love

A daily practice changed my life.
Write it. Say it out loud. Feel it.

TRY THIS:
Each day, list 5 things for
which you give THANKS!
Feel that gratitude in your
body. Where do you feel it?

☆

Noticing **GOOD FEELS** like love, connection, joy?! Savor it!

BraIN Photos!

Brain photos are a way of locking a moment into your brain & body.

Having an awesome day? Capture it with your sight, touch, smell, or taste. Breathe it into your cells.

BREATHE it in. Take a brain/body photo.

Anchor & Embody

Now that you are paying attention —

to your words, thoughts and actions —

it's time for the next step!

Now we PRACTICE dropping the
storyline and **into the body.**

Inhale, heart lifts.

Exhale, round.

Notice the thought.
Let it go.
Ask "what do I need right now?"
Move the body.

Keep breathing.

Today, I need to know...

CUT along dotted lines, RIP and TAKE!

I am
AMAZING!

- -

I am a
Creative
Force!

- -

I am a
Gift.

- -

I am Love(d).

- -

I am Brilliant!

- -

I am
COURAGEOUS.

- -

I am Awesome!

- -

(You can make more!)

Sometimes
we need
someone in
our corner.

I made myself a "Pocket Mum"
to cheer me on, give me
advice, strength and
unconditional love.

You may make your
own Mum — or coach, friend,
guru...whatever you need..

...OR...use mine!

Drop in to your body.

Maybe add some words (mantra):
I AM LOVE.

At my core, I am...

This I know to be TRUE...

When I love myself, I feel...

Write.

Draw.

Dance.

I show me that I love me when I... _____

_____

_____

_____

_____

I lose track of time when I... _____

_____

_____

_____

_____

More than anything, I... _____

_____

_____

_____

_____

_____

(I have more to say...)

When you anchor in
your breath + body,
you may **notice** messages
coming through.

Express

Once you have acknowledged your core/truth/essence...it is your responsibility to

 share it.

Use your voice, body, artistic pursuits, writing...

Get it out!!

The

needs

ewe=you

(The world needs you.)

How I might show up today: ✏️

Energy Moves...
(ideas)

Stretch

Garden

Cry

Walk

Do the wave

Skip

Rip paper

Build a sandcastle

Shower
_____

_____

_____

_____

_____

_____

Cartwheel

Sing

Tap dance

Shake like a dog

Wash dishes
_____

_____

_____

_____

_____

_____

_____

_____

_____

_____

Revisit your Attitude of Gratitude

*and add one
thing each day you
appreciate & celebrate
about YOU!

Keep going...

If I was an inanimate object, I would be...

For me — one day
I painted myself as
a lighthouse!

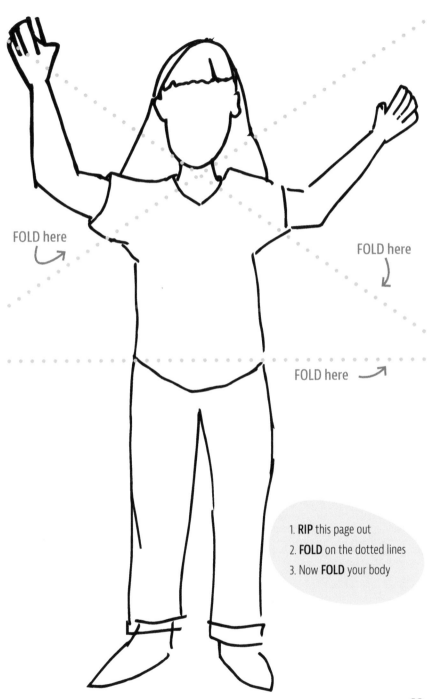

FOLD here

FOLD here

FOLD here

1. **RIP** this page out
2. **FOLD** on the dotted lines
3. Now **FOLD** your body

Be like a rubber band.

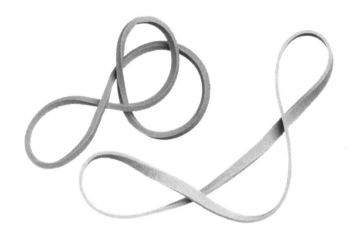

A stretched rubber band is
full of potential (energy) — just like you!

Grab a rubber band.
STRETCH IT.
FLING IT.
SNAP IT.

The leg bone's connected...

Feet, Legs, Hips: They hold you up.
Store feelings of safety, love, home.
Stretch hamstrings to let go...

Shoulders, chest: Carry stress + the weight of the world.
Some **round the shoulders** to protect
the heart.

Spine: Your centerline.
Innervates your system + organs.

Hands: Connects your heart with the world.

...to the hip bone!

 TWISTS — Massages your organs.

 STRAIGHT SPINE — Eases energy + confidence.

 FORWARD FOLD — Calms the body, lowers blood pressure.

 BACKBENDS — Energizes, lifts the heart.

Rest, Renew
& Restore

Allow. Allow. Allow.

Let whatever comes, come. Trust
that you have all you need within.

Breathe long and prosper!

It's ok to snot on this page.
Or doodle it. Or stomp it.
    Or...
      Or...
        Or...

DOODLE page

TRY THIS:

Carefully cut along dots.
Gently pull from center.
Hold page up,
give it a shake!

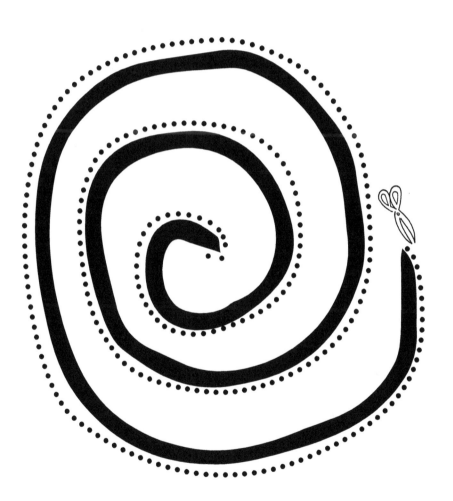

The thing I most want to let go is... ✏️

_____

_____

_____

_____

_____

_____

_____

_____

_____

Tear, cut, or rip on this line.
Once you have written what
you want to release, I invite you
to burn it, bin it, or bury it!

Send it out to the universe
as a prayer. The universe will
handle it from here.

Take a deep breath. Let. It. Go.

Remember that each **EXHALE**
is a practice in letting go.

Palms up to receive.

(Listen.)

REST, REFRESH, REFILL

looks like   to me.

_____

_____

_____

_____

_____

_____

_____

_____

_____

_____

_____

_____

_____

_____

_____

_____

Energy Savers
(a.k.a. Surge Protectors)

> Zip it up.

> Imagine a physical (soft) wall between you + others.

> Take a shower or wash your hands to cleanse your energy.

> Physically **SHAKE IT OFF.**

> Rest. Eat well.

> Keep asking yourself "what do I need right now?"

↓ ↓ ↓

Give yourself what you need.

Zip it up.

1. Stand up.

2. Inhale, sweeping your arms over your head.

3. Exhale, pulling an imaginary zipper down from head to tail.

4. Repeat 3x (or more.)

Breathe.

Write.

Appreciate.

Color.

Move.

How will you rest?

Draw.

SING.

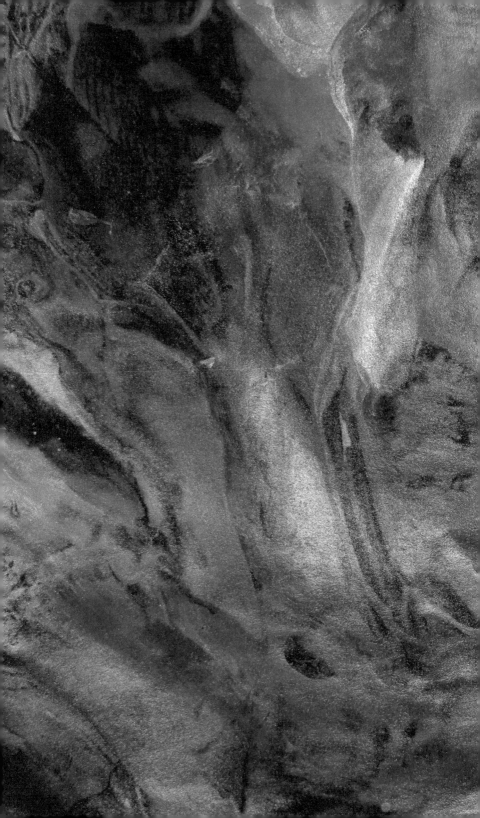

// Between stimulus & response
there is a space.

In that space is our **POWER** to
CHOOSE our response.

In our response lies our **GROWTH**
and our **FREEDOM**. //

ABOUT ANNE L. DAVIS

 Anne digs the human experience. Her work in healthcare focuses on how our perception impacts our health. She believes that the power of health & wellbeing resides within.

Anne is a registered yoga teacher, a leader in meditation and breath work. She serves as the Board President for Sea Change Yoga, offering trauma informed yoga and meditation for all.

Anne loves to write, hike and be outside with her family in Falmouth, Maine.